Your Amazing Itty Bitty™ Gratitude Book

Reduce Stress, Have a Better Life, Boost Your Immune System and Feel Happy

Gratitude is a means by which you can turn your life around.

Since "What you focus on Expands" you get to focus on the things that make you feel good physically, mentally and emotionally.

In this powerful Itty Bitty™ Book, Belinda Lee Cook tells you how to turn the negative thoughts and emotions around so that you can feel positive every day. You will find that, as you use her teachings, your life becomes better and better as you throw off the negatives and embrace the positives.

What Gratitude Does:

- It lessens tension as negatives like anger turn to the positive lessons that anger brings.
- It helps you sleep better as you focus on the positive and release the negative.
- It creates a lasting high of positive energy that releases endorphins as much as running or dark chocolate.

Your Amazing Itty Bitty™ Gratitude Book

15 Simple Steps for Expressing Gratitude in Your Life

Belinda Lee Cook

Published by Itty Bitty Publishing
A subsidiary of S & P Productions, Inc.

Copyright © 2015 Belinda Lee Cook

All rights reserved. No part of this book may be reproduced or transmitted in any form or by any means, electronic or mechanical, including photocopying, recording or by any information storage and retrieval system, without written permission of the publisher, except for inclusion of brief quotations in a review.

Printed in the United States of America

Itty Bitty Publishing
311 Main Street, Suite E
El Segundo, CA 90245
(310) 640-8885

ISBN: 978-1-931191-78-4

Dedication

This book is dedicated to all those people in my life who, through word and deed, showed me how important it is to be grateful for the things, people, and events you've been lucky enough to experience.

Stop by the Itty Bitty™ website to find my interesting blog entries regarding Expressing Gratitude.

www.IttyBittyPublishing.com

Or contact me at

http://belindaleecook.com

Table of Contents

- Step 1. Getting Started
- Step 2. Making a Bad Day Better
- Step 3. Getting a Better Night's Sleep
- Step 4. Turning Anger into Gratitude
- Step 5. Trying a Little Kindness
- Step 6. Meeting Life's Challenges
- Step 7. Focusing on what You Have
- Step 8. Affirming Goodness
- Step 9. Building Lasting High Moments
- Step 10. Blocking Negative Feelings
- Step 11. Busting Stress
- Step 12. Recognizing Someone has Your Back
- Step 13. Giving Credit to Others
- Step 14. Taking Responsibility
- Step 15. Learning Humility

Introduction

In this Itty Bitty Book you will find 15 simple things you can do to express gratitude. Why is this important? Research has shown that the daily practice of being thankful for people, events, and things around you has health benefits. Gratitude boosts your immune system, makes you feel connected to others, banishes depression and makes you feel hopeful.

Step 1
Getting Started

How do you get started? With gratitude, as with everything else you learn, start out with baby steps:

1. Intentionally focus your attention on developing grateful thinking.
2. Once a week, stop and take stock of the good things in your life.
3. In a journal or an electronic file, list five things for which you are grateful that happened during the week.
4. If a negative qualifier or an ungrateful thought comes into your head say to yourself, "Cancel that thought and replace it with three positive thoughts." Even if you can't think of three positive thoughts, just saying that sentence cancels and replaces.
5. Don't just take people, events, and things for granted. Shift your thinking to seeing the gifts in your life.

Getting Started

In the beginning thinking of things to be grateful for can be difficult. We are so accustomed to thinking negatively that complaining actually feels comfortable while gratitude can feel foreign.

- In the beginning, something as simple as getting up on time in the morning can be the focus of gratitude.
- Cooking dinner every night without burning something could be something to be grateful for.
- Getting a new customer for your business could be something to grateful for.
- Taking a twenty-minute walk every day could be something to be grateful for.
- Walking to the end of the driveway could be something to be grateful for.
- The light changing to green just as you get to it can be something to be grateful for.

What in your life can you be grateful for?

Step 2
Making A Bad Day Better

Everybody has bad days. When you're having a particularly trying day there are ways to make it better.

1. The saying goes, "What you focus on expands." If you focus on what you don't have, what you don't have will expand. If you focus on what you do have – even if you only have a little of it – what you do have will grow.
2. Noticing all the things for which you can be thankful will make your bad day better.
3. No matter how bleak things look there are always things you can be grateful for.

Making a Bad Day Better

Focusing on the positive will change your day.

- If a loved one is experiencing health issues, think of ways you can help and then do those things.
- If your teen is being a typical teenager, realize other teens are just like yours. They don't call teens "typical" because what they are doing is unusual. Write down three wonderful things about your teenager that are separate from his or her current behavior. A wonderful thing could be that he took a shower today. That could be a very happy thought.
- Pay someone a compliment out of the blue. The mind has no words for "he, she, it, they and you." The mind hears only "I." When you pay someone else a compliment you make yourself feel good.

Step 3
Getting a Better Night's Sleep

Gratitude helps you sleep better. When you sleep better, your days go better too.

1. Get into the gratitude journal practice.
2. Each night before you go to bed, write in a journal five things you were grateful for during the day. Those things could include people you came in contact with, things that should be ordinary but aren't. Write about little things as well as big things.
3. Be sure to explain why you were grateful for each thing you write down.
4. After you have written in your journal, focus on those things that made you happy as you go to sleep.

Getting a Better Night's Sleep

As you lie in bed waiting to go to sleep, focus your attention on what you wrote in your journal and express your gratitude in your mind.

- Thank you for the rain today. We really needed rain.
- Thank you for my maid.
- Thank for my new car.
- Thank you that my son told me he loved me.

What can you focus on as you go to sleep tonight?

Step 4
Turning Anger into Gratitude

Turn your anger into gratitude. It will make you feel less stressed. It will go a long way toward diffusing a tense, destructive situation.

Instead of getting mad at a co-worker, an employee, a family member, or your neighbor, try this:

1. Bite your tongue (not hard or painfully).
2. Count to ten.
3. Take 10 deep breaths.
4. Think of reasons to be grateful for this person.
5. Focus on what made you grateful not angry.
6. When you are in a good enough mood, show your gratitude to this person who made you angry.
7. Then ask politely if he/she could please refrain from doing whatever made you angry. You will be amazed and delighted with how much better you feel and how much better your request is executed.

More Exercises for Turning Anger into Gratitude

- The first step is to become aware. Finding out more about the situation that is making you angry can be the first step in understanding and moving beyond the anger.
- Don't mitigate your feelings by judging them.
- Tell others when you don't like something and why. Do it in a kind and positive way. Then, forgive them and move on.
- Moving on is the big part. I know people who are still angry at people who have been dead for fifty years. Who does that anger harm? Certainly not the person who has already passed.
- See the goodness in others even when you don't like their actions.
- Look for the gifts in the person and in the situation. Focus on the positives.

Step 5
Trying a Little Kindness

Instead of criticism, try gratitude. You can transform a marriage or child-parent relationship and ease all kinds of stress, tension, and depression by focusing on all the things your wife, parent or child does that make you feel thankful.

1. Instead of nitpicking, carping, nagging, sermonizing, lecturing or criticizing focus on the good things they bring to your life.
2. When you have the urge to criticize, stop. Take a deep, calming breath.
3. Think of all the reasons you're grateful for your spouse, child, parent or sibling.
4. Share that gratitude with them right away.

Your family relationships will be stronger. Your family members will learn from your example and emulate you.

List Five Things to Be Grateful for About the Person Who Most Drives You Crazy.

- At the very least dealing with this person can make you stronger.
- Repeat this exercise for another person or something in your job, house or life.
- Repeat this exercise until nothing bothers you.

Step 6
Meeting Life's Challenges

Life is full of challenges. When things don't go according to plan often people express their frustration in anger, ranting, sorrow, self-pity and complaining.

Turn these challenges into opportunities to become more skilled in every aspect of your life.

1. Be grateful for these opportunities to grow, to learn a new skill, to improve your technique.
2. Express gratitude for the challenges you have been given.
3. Change from being a complainer to a positive person who is up for a challenge.
4. Notice how much easier dealing with challenges becomes.

The Following is a Great Way To Deal with Challenges:

- Write five things you are grateful for about a recent challenge.
- Write five things you notice about how much easier dealing with a challenge becomes after you switch to gratitude.

Step 7
Focusing on What You Have

People bemoan the fact that their lives, careers, or their family are lacking things.

1. Focus instead on all you do have.
2. List talents or abilities for which you are thankful.
3. Write gratitude statements for the things, people, and events you are grateful for. This puts a whole different twist on things.
4. Make a list of comforts you have that may not be afforded to others in other countries.

Make Yourself Aware of What You Have.

- Focus on five things you have for which you are grateful.
- Notice how good this makes you feel.

Be Sure to be Grateful in the Moment.

- If you have been looking for your shoes or your car keys, and you suddenly find them, be sure to express your gratitude.
- You may express it to thin air, to the Creative Universe, to the God you worship.
- Noticing that good things happen and marking them with expressions of gratitude makes you more aware of how many good things there are.

Step 8
Affirming Goodness

Gratitude includes an affirmation of goodness. When you view life as a whole, gratitude encourages you to identify and focus on the goodness in our life.

1. Acknowledging the sources of the goodness around you takes you outside of yourself.
2. True gratitude admits a humble dependence on others—family, colleagues, friends, neighbors, service providers, perhaps even a Higher Power—that has helped you achieve the goodness in your life.

Acknowledge the good things you have for which you are grateful. For example:

- List five gifts you have received.
- List five talents you have.
- List five ways in which you are lucky.
- List five benefits you have received in your life.
- Express gratitude for the source of the goodness.

Step 9
Building Lasting High Moments

Gratitude helps you appreciate the value and thus extract more benefits from the good things in life.

1. Gratitude allows a deeper participation in life.
2. You become more sharply aware of the positives. This allows you to sustain feelings of excitement.
3. This magnifies the pleasures of the moment and builds more lasting memories of those high moments.

If Something Wonderful Happens Stop and Take a Minute To Celebrate It.

If you do not notice the good things why should they continue to happen? Remember "What you focus on expands."

- Whenever something good happens no matter how big or small stop what you are doing and celebrate.
- Celebration can look like a high-five.
- Celebration can take the form of calling a friend and sharing your excitement.

Step 10
Blocking Negative Feelings

Being grateful blocks negative emotions like jealousy, greed, envy, regret, anger and resentment.

1. Stop each day and be grateful for what you have. When you are being grateful for what you have, it's almost impossible to focus on what others have that you don't or what you think should rightfully have been yours.
2. You cannot be grateful and envious at the same time.
3. Negative feelings like resentment and anger are toxic to your physical, mental, emotional and social well-being. They can destroy your happiness.

A study by Dr. Alex Wood in the *Journal of Research in Personality (2008)*, demonstrated that gratitude can cut the severity, duration, and frequency of episodes of depression.

Exercises for Gratitude:

- Get in the habit of noticing positive things.
- Take time to meditate on the things you are grateful for.

Step 11
Busting Stress

People who are grateful are more resistant to stress, trauma, adversity and suffering. In short:

1. Gratitude gives people a positive perspective to interpret negative life events and guard against post-traumatic stress and anxiety.
2. They recover from those tough times in their lives more quickly.
3. They are more resilient.
4. They are mentally, physically and emotionally healthier.

Practice Gratitude Every Day.

- List 10 things in your life for which you are grateful.
- Express gratitude for each of them at least once a day for 21-Days.

Step 12
Recognize that Someone Has Your Back

Grateful people have a greater sense of self-worth.

1. When you are grateful, you feel as if others are looking out for you and have your best interests at heart. Somebody—person or higher power—has your back.
2. When you begin to recognize the contributions of others, you see that they value you.
3. Few of you get where you want to go all by yourselves. Become aware not only of the contributions other people make to your lives but how you could ask them to help you even more. People love helping other people.

Become Acutely Aware that "No Man is an Island".

- Stop and be grateful for the people around you and what they do for you.
- Be aware of a network of past and present people who have helped and are helping you get where you are.
- Become aware of the ways in which you can contribute to the lives of others and enjoy the feeling of gratitude that gives you.

Step 13
Giving Credit to Others

When you succeed at something, be sure to include others in your expressions of gratitude.

1. Acknowledge those people, events, and things that helped in your achievement of what you want.
2. Give credit to others for your success: parents, teachers, colleagues, employees, siblings, even God.
3. Thank others publicly and privately for their input.
4. Pay it forward. Help others as you were helped.
5. Look for ways to use your time and talents to assist others.

It's Important To Express Gratitude to Those Who Have Helped Your Succees.

- List those who have helped you succeed, and to whom you are grateful.
- Express the contribution of each.

Step 14
Taking Responsibility

Gratitude focuses on the positive in every situation even those that might at first appear negative.

1. Avoid blaming other people and events for things that did not go well.
2. Accept the responsibility for how things turned out.
3. Learn from each experience.

Turn Arounds

- Write about something that did not turn out the way you had hoped it would.
- List five ways in which you benefitted from the experience.
- Rewrite your description of what happened as an expression of gratitude incorporating those benefits into the situation.

Step 15
Gratitude Develops Humility

Gratitude fosters humility.

1. When you are riding high on success it is easy to forget the people, things and/or events that helped you get there.
2. If you take time to consider the people, things and/or events that contributed to your success, it makes you grateful for luck, help, and support that got you where you are.
3. When you are thankful for small things like a safe home, a shelter from the cold, a hot meal, someone who cares about you, it is easy to become filled with gratitude and humility.

Humility Exercise

- In your gratitude journal, acknowledge the humility that your gratitude causes.
- List the "creature comforts" that make your life enjoyable.
- List the talents, skills and abilities which you feel lucky to possess.
- Acknowledge the help and support that family members have given you.
- Describe how friends have helped you arrive where you are.
- List the co-workers who have contributed to your success.
- List everything else not \preciously mentioned.

Meditate on your lists at the end of each day.
Keep building these lists and expressing gratitude first thing in the morning and last thing at night.

You've Finished! But, before You Go…

Tweet/share that you finished this book.

Please star rate this book.

Reviews are solid gold to writers. Please take a few minutes to give us some itty bitty feedback on this book and post it on the site from which you bought the book.

ABOUT THE AUTHOR

Belinda Lee Cook is a serial entrepreneur by trade. A voracious reader and writer, writing and research are her passion. It should come as no surprise, then, that she is a huge fan of Itty Bitty Books. There is so much practical information packed into a small space.

She was fortunate to have work she loved, employees whom she cherished, colleagues whom she admired, a mentor whom she loved and children who taught her daily the joy of learning and caring for others. These friends, colleagues and children, ages five to ninety-five, reminded her that she has been successful because of the people, events, and things with whom she has been fortunate to rub shoulders.

Finding a career where you look forward to going to work each day is a blessing. Belinda has been twice blessed. When she retired, selling a Chevron Gas Station, she took up traveling, reading and writing. Through the pursuit of traveling in particular she has met some wonderful people from all over the world. They have become lifelong friends.

William Arthur Ward said, "Gratitude can transform common days into thanksgivings, turn routine jobs into joy and change ordinary opportunities into blessings." Belinda leaves her readers with this apt message and her gratitude!

http://belindaleecook.com

Other Amazing Itty Bitty™ Books

- **Your Amazing Itty Bitty™ Astrology Book** – Carol Pilkington

- **Your Amazing Itty Bitty™ Heal Your Body Book** – Patricia Garza Pinto

- **Your Amazing Itty Bitty™ Book Of Empowerment Through Hope** – LeAnna Blackmon

With many more Amazing Itty Bitty Books available online and in paperback.

www.ingramcontent.com/pod-product-compliance
Lightning Source LLC
Chambersburg PA
CBHW061304040426
42444CB00010B/2513